Grampian
Regional Council

GRAMPIAN'S PAST

Its Archaeology from the Air

Ian A G Shepherd & Moira K Greig

1996

Cessna 152, the classic aerial platform.

Aviation history: Cairnhall Hangar, Kintore; built 1935 for Ted Freeson's Highland Airways which flew from the adjacent field.

Cover:
Vertical view in winter of a late prehistoric enclosure on Stot Hill, Lumphanan, surrounded by forestry ploughing, taken 1990.

Title Page:
Cropmark of a prehistoric enclosure with two entrances at Pitcarry, Inverbervie, taken 1991.

Grampian
Regional Council

RCAHMS

Grampian Regional Council is grateful to the Royal Commission on the Ancient and Historical Monuments of Scotland for both supporting flying costs over the years and for making a grant towards this publication; and to Dr Ian Ralston for his unstinting commitment and expertise during the early years of the flying programme.

Published by the Economic Development & Planning Department of Grampian Regional Council, Aberdeen, 1996.
Printed on environmentally responsible paper by Gilcomston Litho Ltd Aberdeen.
British Library Cataloguing in Publication Data. A catalogue record for this book is available from the British Library.
ISBN 0 9464 49 06 6

foreword

In 1975 the newly-formed Grampian Regional Council was the first Regional authority in Scotland to appoint a Regional Archaeologist. This began a commitment to both the protection and the interpretation of the ancient built heritage of the region that has developed and strengthened over the years.

In particular, through the programme of aerial reconnaissance which began in 1977, and to 1984 ran in partnership with the Lecturer in Archaeology in the University of Aberdeen, came a growing appreciation of the richness and variety of the many historic landscapes of Grampian. In order to further understanding of one group of cropmarks, the Council's Heritage Fund was used to fund the excavation in 1990 of one of the pit-circles at Bellie, Fochabers, establishing that it had been a substantial Iron-Age house.

We are certain that the depth of time represented by the stunning images presented here will be both a revelation and a lasting record.

Gordon MacDonald
Convener

The Grampian landscape looking south towards Bennachie, taken from just south of Banff.

Dunnottar Castle, Stonehaven,
ground and aerial views.

The lower photograph of the castle is taken on the ground. You are aware it is perched on a cliff but it is only in the illustration above that you can fully appreciate its magnificent setting. The eye can now take in a wider area and understand the powerful defensive position of the site.

The great cliff-girt plateau was very probably fortified in the early historic period; it is most likely the *Dun Fother* of the Irish annals, besieged in AD 683. The earliest structure extant on the promontory is the keep of the Earl Marischal, visible in the bottom right of the photograph. The scale of the plateau allowed an unusually extensive range of buildings to be developed in the 16th century. These form the great Quadrangle visible in the top left, adjacent to the chapel. The massive L-shaped bank at the bottom left was erected as a defence from Cromwell's artillery during the siege of 1652.

Why do archaeologists fly ?

When Grampian Regional Council established its Archaeological Service in 1975, the first imperative was to build up an archaeological Sites and Monuments Record. This required as much information as possible on archaeological sites throughout the region. In order to discover previously unrecorded sites throughout the vast area of Grampian the technique of archaeological aerial reconnaisance was employed from 1977. The work began initially in collaboration with Dr Ian Ralston of the Geography Department, University of Aberdeen, but since 1984 it has been the sole responsibility of the Regional Archaeological Service. In this work, the flying costs were borne initially by the Inspectorate of Ancient Monuments (Scottish Development Department) and for the last ten years by the Royal Commission on the Ancient and Historical Monuments of Scotland. In all more than 800 previously unrecorded sites have been photographed. The Service has therefore built up a considerable collection of aerial photographs over the years. This book contains a selection of these photographs to show the wealth of archaeological sites and landscapes that exist in Grampian.

For over six thousand years people have left evidence of their use of the land, from great cairns erected as burial sites, to traces of their farming activity. As well as these visible remains there are also many hidden archaeological sites which are only revealed under particular conditions and at certain times in the year.

From the ground only a certain area of an archaeological site is visible at one time. By changing the viewpoint, by taking to the air, the eye is given greater scope, and an appreciation of the shape and landscape setting of the site can be gained. In some cases the sites are only visible from the air and nothing can be seen on the ground even when one is standing on them.

Flights take place all the year round. Upstanding sites, such as harbours, castles, stone circles, etc are recorded at any time, but different seasons and weather conditions reveal other types of sites.

By late spring and early summer crops of barley, oats and wheat have become well established. This can be one of the most exciting times to fly as cropmark sites are beginning to appear. Weather plays a very large part in the formation of cropmarks. Ideally archaeologists look for a dry spring and summer to allow the marks to "set" in the growing crops.

The term "cropmark" refers to a difference in crop growth which is visible especially from the air. Such a difference can indicate features lying beneath the ground. When people built structures in the prehistoric and early historic periods, they dug holes into the sub-soil to place structural posts. Enclosures, banked and ditched, and stockades were dug to protect homes and animals. Pits were dug to bury the dead. Over time the huts decayed, were removed or even destroyed. The timber rotted and the holes and ditches slowly filled with soil. As a result in subsequent years there would be a greater depth of soil in the areas which had been disturbed. This means that crops sown on the site of these structures will develop roots which are longer and better nourished. The consequent stronger growth relative to the rest of the crop shows the shape of the original structure from the air.

Gordon Schools, Huntly,
designed by Archibald Simpson, 1839-41

In a dry season the greater depth of soil retains moisture longer than the shallower areas which become stressed, resulting in some startlingly clear sites. We know from some excavated sites that many more features survive under the ground than appear on the aerial photographs.

If, in contrast, the walls were built of stone, there is a lesser depth of soil where surviving foundations lie. This results in poorer crop growth above the site. After a long dry spell parch-marks will start to show, taking on the shape of the buried structure.

Different crops can also affect the results. Cereal crops such as barley, oats and wheat show best of all, although wheat, with its hard straight stalk, is not quite so revealing. Oil-seed rape, turnips, beet and potatoes generally do not show anything, unless under exceptionally dry conditions.

The cropmarks appear as a variety of circles, ovals, rectangular shapes and linear features reflecting the underlying archaeology. We have attempted to give a brief description of

Greshop, Forres, from the air. The broad dark green trace is a fossil river. There are archaeological features on either side. The ground picture, below, was taken from the point where the track joins the main road.

The same site from ground level; distinct colour changes can be seen in the growing barley.

what these represent and the period to which they belong, although much research and excavation remain to be done in order to confirm these attributions.

In winter the vegetation dies down. This in itself can reveal new features or enable a known site to stand out better. The lower angle of winter sun-light throws longer shadows across the ground, emphasising slight banks and humps which are not normally visible. The remains of deserted settlements, rig and furrow (the remains of strip cultivation carried out in medieval times), and also prehistoric field systems (enclosures and small cairns) can then be seen. These survive best in upland areas where subsequent land use has been sufficiently light to allow the features to remain.

A fall of snow can greatly enhance our understanding of the landscape by blocking out the intrusions of differing vegetation or other land cover. If lit by strong, low-angled sunlight any banks and hollows can create dramatic shadows and contrasts. The rendering of the landscape in black and white oftens lends a sense of timelessness to photographs. This is especially good for showing up prehistoric field systems, which survive on unimproved ground as sinuous narrow banks and small cairns, which are stone clearance heaps.

Because of ever-changing conditions the most productive areas for cropmarks are flown over more than once each year: ie

2 The same landscape in summer; the confusion of textures and colours reveals much less.

the Mearns, the Garioch and the coastal plain of Moray. Very dry weather can reveal a site to be much more extensive than appeared when it was first photographed. Even in the same year an early summer flight can have very different results from a later summer flight, while the rare combination of light snow cover and strong sun can produce a startling number of new sites from a single winter flight.

The results of the aerial archaeology programme presented in this book enhance our knowlege of the true extent of the human impact on the landscape of Grampian Region over the millennia.

This book is laid out in chronological order, starting from the last World War and going back to the times of the first farmers, in the Neolithic period, some 6000 years ago. The principal features of archaeological interest in each photograph are described in the caption, along with the place-name. A small map on each double spread also shows the general location of each site. A brief catalogue of all photographs is given at the back of the book.

1 Golf course, Aboyne, under snow; showing how a combination of snow cover and strong sun can reveal upstanding earthworks such as these sinuous strips of medieval rig and furrow cultivation.

1 • 2

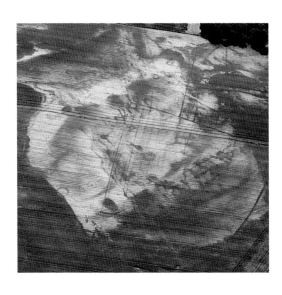

Features from the recent past, such as World War II instalations, are of archaeological importance and can be studied from the air.

3 Midtown, Elgin. The two circular features in the left of centre are probably traces of searchlight batteries from the war-time use of the adjacent airfield. The straight marks are recent man-made boundaries and drains. The dramatic curvilinear features reflect the variegated sub-soil, with later prehistoric archaeological features interspersed.

4 Rattray Airfield, north of Peterhead, on the edge of the Loch of Strathbeg; used during the last war as an operational training base for young naval pilots who had just gained their wings. Now covered with radio masts.

6 Slate quarries on Hill of Foudland, Gordon - an important source for the north-east in the late 18th and 19th centuries.

Quarrying and other extractive processes have made their vivid impacts on the Grampian landscape.

5 Rubislaw Quarry, Aberdeen, which supplied granite to much of Aberdeen and throughout the world, in 1978, not long after its closure. It remains one of the largest man-made holes in the world.

7 Mechanical extraction of peat at Rora Moss, St Fergus, 1994.

8 St Cyrus; traces of the Montrose to Inverbervie branch railway line, 1861-5, which was an essential factor in the success of the flax mills of Inverbervie and the fishing of Gourdon and Johnshaven in the second half of the 19th century.

9 Burghead Harbour, Moray, built 1807-10 by Thomas Telford who also designed the fine warehouses. The adjacent grid-plan village was built from 1805.

11 The west end of the medieval burgh of Elgin in 1978 with the royal castle of Ladyhill in the foreground - showing the classic medieval layout of long rigs or plots to the left side of the High Street, since obscured by the building of Alexandra Road.

Above left
10 Archiestown, Moray - a village founded by Archibald Grant (1760) which retains its regular, planned layout.

12 The royal burgh of Inverbervie, Kincardine, established on a knoll above the Bervie Water and the sea. The church of 1837 and the two bridges of 1777 and 1935 carrying the main north/south road are clearly visible. Taken 1991.

Grampian has a rich heritage of country houses surviving in various states of repair.

Left
15 The cliff-top location of the new Slains Castle, rebuilt 1836-7, by John Smith, the Aberdeen architect.

Below
16 Duff House, Banff - designed by William Adam (1735-49) for William Duff, Earl Fife; recently restored by Historic Scotland as a country house gallery, an outpost of the National Galleries of Scotland, managed by Banff and Buchan District Council and Grampian Regional Council.

Above
14 The Jacobean fantasy of Ecclesgreig House, St Cyrus, built 1844 by architect Henry Edmund Goodridge of Bath, Somerset.

Centre
17 Cairness House, a neo-classical house designed by James Playfair, 1791-7. An exceptional house of outstanding merit.

Cairness House from above.

Left
13 The planned town of Fochabers on the River Spey in Moray - laid out in a grid plan in 1776 adjacent to the policies of Gordon Castle, as the old village next to a castle was deemed to be too close to the landowner, the Duke of Gordon.

18 Corgarff Castle, Strathdon; built as a simple towerhouse in 1537, it was converted to a Hanoverian garrison in 1748 by enclosing it within a star-shaped curtain wall, for defence by muskets.

19 Keith Hall; the final plan of this *large and stately mansion*, of the later Scottish Renaissance, designed c1662-1700, is clear from the air.

20 Huntly Castle: both the great Renaissance palace of Huntly and parts of the two preceding castles are visible from the air. The 12th-century Peel of Strathbogie can be partly seen as a grassy mound to the left of the castle, while the L-plan foundations of *the great olde tower* of c1400 are visible behind the palace. The palace itself, which was one of the most lavish houses of the second half of the 16th century in Scotland, had the private chambers of the Earl of Gordon in the great round tower and fine oriel windows of French inspiration on the main block.

17

22 Doolie Bridge, Fyvie. The slopes above the River Ythan were too steep to interest the 19th-century improvers. A relict landscape survives in these marginal areas which gives us some idea how busy the pre-improvement landscape would have been. An old track winds its way down from the top centre, passing a longhouse, yard and cultivation terrace. At the bottom of the slope three longhouses lie at the river's edge, between two enclosures. The small circular feature forward of the main terrace may be the remains of a prehistoric house. There are also indeterminate traces of cultivation in the bracken below the terrace.

19

Left
21 Ardlair, Kennethmont: landscape history as geometry. The large regular fields around the edge of the picture were laid out in the 19th century by the agricultural improvers. An *island* was left, the circular enclosure in the centre, in which trees were planted over medieval rig & furrow cultivation. The plantation bank has truncated the rigs, which are clearly visible running up and over the hill. A much earlier monument, a recumbent stone circle of c 5000 years ago, is visible on the hill-top, left of centre. All this is revealed by a fortunate combination of sun and snow.

.**22**

21.

24 Tillygarmond, Finzean: low autumn sun throws up the houses and yards of a pre-improvement settlement criss-crossed by modern tracks.

Left
23 Eslie, Strachan: the 19th-century farmstead with its traditional open courtyard surrounded by regular, blank fields is mirrored by its predecessor across the road. Low winter sun and snow reveal the foundations of the pre-improvement farmhouse (centre) and its yards and other buildings. The tiny circle to the right of the small quadrangular enclosure is a whin mill used for crushing whin for cattle feed.

24.•23

25 Near-vertical winter view of a pre-improvement farmstead on Breda Hill, Alford, which has partly survived in rough ground beside a modern field. The house is in the centre of the picture.

26 Water of Dye: the gentle slopes on either side of the Water of Dye were once alive with agriculture, as shown by these pre-improvement fields and houses. The modern track up to Glen Dye reservoir snakes through the rectangular fields which are showing under a light snow cover.

25.

26.

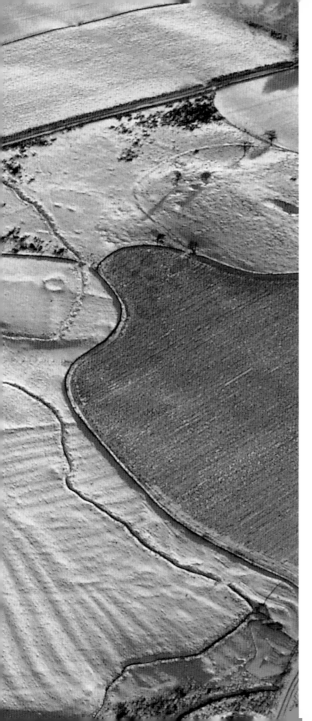

28 Wood of Schivas, on the Ythan, has retained the medieval pattern of rig cultivation because the area went into trees in the late 18th century, when the surrounding landscape was double-dug and the modern fields created. The little circular feature and the stone dykes are later than the medieval cultivation.

Left
27 A rare example of a medieval farm at Wardhouse, Kennethmont. In the right centre are the low platforms of the farm buildings and tracks from which the sinuous cultivation rigs fan out. An earlier, prehistoric, phase in the upper centre is represented by two circular houses and a group of small cairns.

27. .28

29 Glen Muick, Deeside: deep agricultural terracing is visible on the right, adjacent to the stone work of an extensive later deserted settlement. More is visible under snow (No. 30).

30 Sunlight is not essential for winter flying. This almost monochrome shot of Glen Muick shows how melting snow can enhance the recognition of archaeological features. In this case the snow has gone from the upstanding cultivation rigs but remains in the lower-lying, colder, furrows. The intensity of occupation and former cultivation of this glen is thus vividly revealed.

31 Snow reveals part of the 13th-century Deer Dyke which confined the King's deer in his hunting park above the royal seat of Kincardine Castle. A line of modern grouse butts can be seen to the left of, and parallel to, the bank. The broad clear strips are produced by the heather-burning required to maintain the grouse moor.

29,30   .31

33 Fedderate Castle, Maud: built by the Crawfords in 1474, extended 1519; beseiged after the Battle of Cromdale (1690). It was blown up in an attempt to clear the ground for agriculture in the 19th century.

32 Clinging to the cliffs of a coastal promontory near Sandend are the remains of the palace block of Findlater Castle which was occupied from the 14th century to 1600 as the seat of the Ogilvies.

35 Duffus Castle, Moray: the prominent mound of the 12th-century motte (which was later crowned by the stone castle in the 14th century) is visible in the right hand corner of the large enclosure, or bailey. When this was built the surrounding land would have been very marshy and ill-drained.

34 The great 13th-century castle and enclosure of Kildrummy, surrounded by a broad ditch. The elaborate gatehouse, modelled on Welsh examples and built c1296, and the massive Warden's tower are clearly visible.

37 Rather more of Wardhouse is revealed in this early summer cropmark which shows the broad encircling ditch surrounded by the narrower ditch of an outer enclosure. An adjacent enclosure can be seen on the right.

36 The ditch of the 13th-century Castle of Wardhouse, Kennethmont is revealed by snow and sunlight; the castle was destroyed in 1647 and finally became erased by farming. The black diamond shape is a water-logged hollow.

39 The promontory of Gardiebane can be seen jutting into the frozen loch. At its neck are two banks and a ditch which may be of medieval date.

38 Loch Kinord, with Castle Island, the site of an early timber castle, later replaced in stone by the *Mansion of Lochcanmour*, mentioned 1511. In 1646, during *the Trubles*, it was restored and garrisoned in the royalist interest by the Marquis of Huntly; it was then beseiged by General David Leslie and thoroughly slighted in 1648. The island was connected to the land by a complex timber structure which was removed in 1783 and used to bridge the Dee at Ballater before it was swept away in the flood of 1789. The little islet to the left of centre is a crannog or lake dwelling of probable Iron-Age date (2000 years ago). At top right is the promontory of Gardiebane, visible in the snow photo on the right.

36.37

38 . 39

41 Pluscarden Abbey: the peaceful setting of this now-restored 13th-century abbey, in its vale south of Elgin, can be recognised easily. Pluscarden was founded in 1230 by Alexander II as one of only three Valliscaulian priories in Scotland, but became a Benedictine house in 1454, on uniting with the Priory of Urquhart. Its glorious restoration, since 1948, is being achieved by a community of Benedictine monks.

42 Deer Abbey: the ground-plan of this Cistercian Abbey (founded c1218 by William Comyn, Earl of Buchan) is evident in this winter shot. The cruciform church and the cloisters immediately to its right are particularly visible.

Left
40 The unusual, sub-triangular, shape of the medieval motte of the Peel of Fichlie, Strathdon, as well as the elements of its landscape can be readily appreciated in this winter photograph. A timber tower and palisade would have been built on the flat summit of the earthwork.

41.
. 42
40 .

43 The circular enclosure wall surrounding the roofless, late medieval, Tullich Kirk, Ballater, hints at a much earlier origin. The large number of early Christian grave slabs still to be seen here confirms it as one of the first Christian sites in Grampian, founded perhaps as early as the 7th or 8th century AD. It is traditionally associated with St Nathalan's mission amongst the Picts.

44 Hills of Boyndie, Banff; a possible Pictish burial complex represented by cropmarks of at least two square barrows (mounds) and three circular barrows.

44
•

43 •

45 A cropmark landscape, rare in Grampian, at Greshop, west of Forres, Moray. The very broad dark green marks are the traces of old river channels. (The *vein* pattern of modern tile drainage can be seen running along them.) In the upper centre the short diagonal lines are remains of medieval rig & furrow ploughing. The five circular traces in a line at right centre are most likely to be Iron-Age houses (although they might also be interpreted as the remains of Bronze-Age burial mounds). The large square trace, bottom left, has gaps in its corners and encloses another square, also with gaps in its corners. Between it and the field boundary are other squares with central pits. These can be interpreted as Pictish burials of the first millennium AD, although the larger feature is clearly more elaborate. There are other miscellaneous marks (eg bottom centre and extreme right) which may relate to the use of this area as a training airfield in the last war.

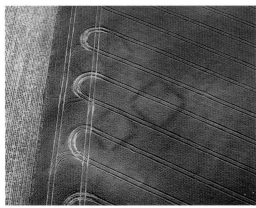

46 Pitairlie, Elgin: cropmarks of at least five small square barrows (mounds) which may represent Pictish burial sites.

47 Cullykhan, Castle Point, Troup. Low winter sunlight raking over this coastal promontory shows many phases of occupation, running back in time. Fort Fiddes, an 18th-19th-century artillery fort lies at the top of the picture, with the medieval focus in the centre. The excavation trenches of Colvin Greig in the 1970s, in the foreground, reveal the Pictish and Iron-Age occupations of the promontory, including a defensive wall on the left side of the enclosure.

48 Green Castle, Portknockie: a coastal promontory adjacent to the 19th-century fishing village of Portknockie. Excavation, by Dr Ian Ralston, 1976-1981, established that this was defended several times from the 6th century BC to the 9th century AD. The excavation trenches can be seen clearly on the upper summit; traces of a Pictish wall run round the upper (far), edge. In the 19th century the promontory was used for net- and fish-drying.

49 Craig Dorney, Glass: the single circuit of ditch and bank surrounding a craggy summit may belong to the Pictish period (mid first millennium AD).

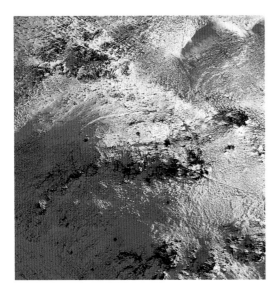

50 Mither Tap o'Bennachie, Garioch: the two stone walls which surround the tor at the top of Bennachie stand out well. The arrangement of upper and lower enclosures suggests that this fort is Pictish in date.

51 Dundarg, Aberdour; the defensive potential of this coastal promontory can be understood well, owing to the strong, angled, sunlight which picks out traces of late medieval structures on the promontory. The earlier defences of the Iron-Age and Pictish fort are visible in the foreground, represented by parallel ditches and banks and a green strip running from the break in the enclosure wall at centre left. The house was built in 1938.

52 This strongly back-lit view of the Hill of Dunnideer, near Insch, reveals a complex defended site, evidence for whose use spans more than 2000 years. The medieval castle (c AD 1260), one of the earliest stone castles on the Scottish mainland, sits within an upper oval enclosure formed by a stone and timber wall of later prehistoric date. This wall at some time had been set on fire and burned so fiercely that its stones vitrified, or fused, together. This upper fort is surrounded by an outer terrace, below which, centre left, can be seen three small platforms scooped out of the slope. These may be medieval in date. The prominent green patch on the left shoulder of the hill is the platform created for a house site of the early or mid first millennium BC. Further along the slope, on the right, are the earth circuits of yet another defensive phase, possibly unfinished. The characteristic ribs of medieval rig & furrow cultivation survive in the left of the picture. Dunnideer remains as an archaeological island in the midst of modern fields.

52

53 Strathhowe, Pennan: the deeply incised dens of the Tore of Troup were formed by water melting from the overlying glacier at the end of the last Ice Age. They provided a perfect defensive opportunity for this little, later prehistoric fort, represented by two parallel ditches dug across the neck of the promontory. They are visible owing to land reclamation for farming in the 1980s.

54 Burghead, Moray: remains of the largest fort in Pictish times (c300 - 900 AD) in Scotland. Findspot of the famous Burghead Bull symbol stones. Although most of the earthworks were removed when the 19th-century village was built, this gently back-lit view shows the remaining ramparts, defining the upper and lower wards, and the Doorie Hill (centre left). This mound, on which the Clavie is burnt each year on the *Auld E'el*, 11th January (the New Year of the previous calendar), is all that survives of the three massive ramparts which were built right across the promontory, possibly in Iron-Age times.

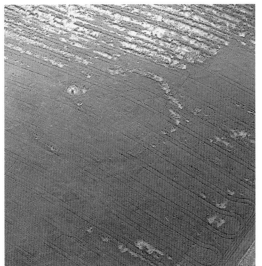

Single aerial photographs can never provide all the information on a site.

55 Barflat, Rhynie: this view was taken in 1978, shortly after the discovery in this field of the Pictish stone known as the Rhynie Man. Another Pictish stone, *The Craw Stane*, can be seen in the left centre of the photograph. It stands just within the circumference of a broad ditch showing faintly in a tashed crop of oats.

56 Regular flying has built up a suite of photographs of this site; this photograph, taken in early July 1992, shows a multi-period enclosure with an internal ditch or palisade, other internal sub-divisions, and annexes. Survey continues.

54   53

55 56

44

57 Deer's Den, Kintore: the single line running diagonally across the centre of this picture represents the ditch of the Roman temporary camp. The *titulum*, or traverse, a short ditch dug outside the entrance to guard against a rush attack, can be seen well. Such camps can be over 40 ha in extent and date from the late first or early third centuries AD. Taken in 1995.

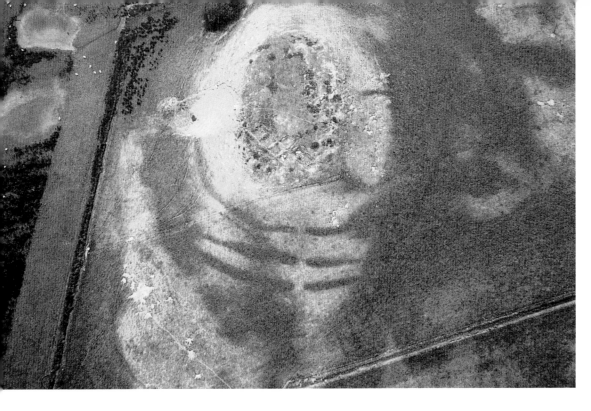

58 Greencairn fort, Cairnton of Balbegno: occupying a low gravel knoll in the Mearns near Fettercairn. Traces of a small stone-walled oval fort of the late first millennium BC can be seen on the summit (the grid pattern is the remains of an old archaeological excavation). The very dry summer of 1989 burnt the grass off the knoll and revealed a previously unknown defensive phase of three concentric ditches with entrance gaps. This fort is in a low-lying, previously boggy, location.

59 Part of the circuit of a very large Roman temporary camp at Durno, Pitcaple. The ditch is angled, with a *titulum* (traverse) clearly visible. The existence of this very large camp, of 55 ha, opposite Bennachie, has led to the suggestion that the Battle of Mons Graupius, AD 84, in which the Romans subdued the Caledonians, took place near here.

60 Durn Hill, Portsoy: most of the plan of this unfinished fort of the first millennium BC can be seen in rough pasture. The most complete part is shown by the bank of whin in the distance, but two circuits of concentric marking-out trenches can be discerned in the foreground. It is not now believed that such unfinished forts were abandoned in the face of an advancing Roman army.

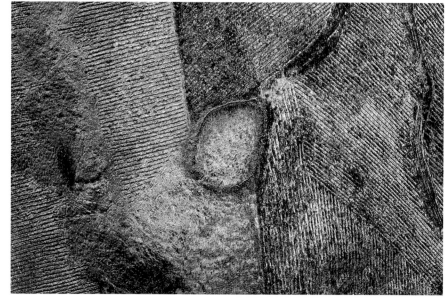

61 Stot Hill, Lumphanan; vertical view of a later prehistoric stone-walled enclosure surrounded by forestry. The radical nature of the landscape change that forestry represents is manifest. This planting was designed under a less archaeologically-friendly grant scheme than pertains today. It is now possible to safeguard more of the setting of such important field monuments.

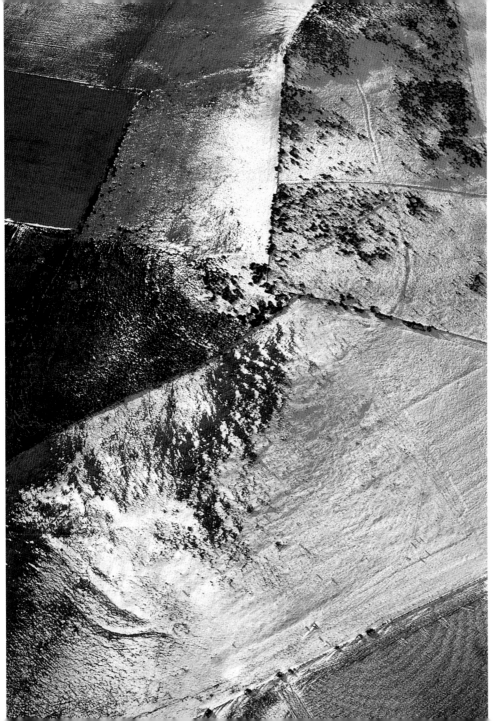

62 Hill of New Leslie, Insch: the impact of differing land uses on earthwork archaeology is clearly seen in this view of the hillfort of New Leslie. The circuit of ditch and banks stands out well in the unimproved ground on the right of the picture (the less hospitable north-facing slope), whereas in the middle right, and the upper left of the picture, the hill has been taken into cultivation and the defences of the fort are consequently much more difficult to trace.

60

62

61

63 Barmekin of Echt: at least two phases of first-millennium BC defence are visible on this hill top. The inner double ring of stones represents a pair of strong walls which augmented the earlier, triple, circuit of earthen ramparts and ditches which now lie in the heather. Remarkably little survives of the late 19th-century observatory which lay within the interior of the fort.

64 Tap o'Noth, Rhynie: the great upper fort, the second highest hillfort in Scotland (at 563m), is revealed from the air as a rectangular area enclosed by a truly massive wall which has collapsed. This wall was originally constructed from stone with timber baulks running through it, to create a defence more than 6m in height. At some date in later prehistory this fort was captured and set on fire. This caused a massive conflagration in which the stones fused together. Traces of this "vitrification" can be seen, top left, between the trig point and the old fire tower.

49

65 Tap o'Noth: this winter shot shows not only the dominating upper fort but also the stone wall of a very large enclosure snaking around the upper slopes of the hill. This wall encloses a very sizeable 21 hectares; traces of house platforms and quarries remain inside its circuit. The elevation and size of this fort suggest that it may date from as early as the beginning of the first millennium BC.

64 65

These two stone-walled enclosures occupy low hills forward of the Bennachie range. They are most likely to belong to the second half of the first millennium BC, and have survived because the 19th-century farmers did not think them worth clearing for cultivation.

66 The Tillymuick enclosure contains the footings of several later prehistoric round houses. The radial pattern is caused by cutting dense whin.

67 There are two longhouses, centre right, in the Berryhill enclosure, indicating reuse of the hilltop in late medieval times. This enclosure forms part of the Archaeolink archaeological park at Oyne.

51

Later prehistoric enclosures were also made of timber.

69 West Balhalgardy, Inverurie: traces of a roughly circular stockade are represented by a very fine, slightly irregular cropmark in the centre of the picture. This may represent a single farmstead.

68 Newton of Lewesk, Pitcaple. Occupying the top of a low ridge is the cropmark of a rectangular enclosure; it probably represents an Iron-Age farm of c 2000 years ago, revealed by a combination of colour contrasts and differential crop growth, enhanced by back-lighting.

70 Mains of Balfour, Birse: the fine cropmark detail of an apparently unenclosed settlement of the late first millennium BC or early first millennium AD. The single L-shape and two banana-shapes are traces of souterrains or underground store-houses. The souterrain at the centre right can be seen to be emerging from a very large timber house represented by two arcs of post-pits (the outer ring is incomplete).

71 The same site at a later stage in the development of a crop. This near-vertical shot shows in greater detail how the marks *reverse out* as the crop nears maturity. The three souterrains and the pit circles now show as silvery-white against the dusty brown of the cereal crop.

72 Romancampgate, Bellie, Fochabers: near-vertical view of Gordon Barclay's excavation in 1990, sponsored by Grampian Regional Council, which was carried out to determine the nature and date of a series of similar pit-circle cropmarks. The excavation established that the pits represent the post-holes of several phases of a massive timber round house of the third or second century BC, very similar in plan to the structure on the opposite page.

73 Burnhead of Monboddo, Laurencekirk: traces of a heavily ploughed late prehistoric settlement on a low gravel ridge in the Mearns. The crops, where the soil is thin on the gravel ridge, have changed colour faster than in the surrounding fields, revealing circular timber houses (right), outbuildings, and other features including possible souterrains in centre left, dug into the subsoil.

72.

70 71

73

74 Logie, Pitcaple: this circular cropmark indicates a small ditched enclosure with a gap for an entrance at the far side. It may have enclosed a timber house similar to Braehead, below.

75 Braehead, Monymusk: an unusual parchmark produced in the dry summer of 1989. It shows the very narrow wall of a large timber house of the first millennium BC, enclosed by a neat circular ditch. The paired post-holes at the entrance to the house are just discernible.

77 Aboyne, Deeside: a remarkably similar version of the Braehead house (no 75), indicated by a very narrow circular trace of the wall surrounded by a wide ditch. There is a causeway across the ditch on the right.

76 Dallachy, Moray: the three circular early cropmarks in the lower centre are best interpreted as later prehistoric houses similar to those on the opposite page. There is also a square barrow at the top of the picture, which may represent a Pictish burial.

78 Creaganducy, Finzean: a survival of an unusual settlement and field system of the first millennium BC. Two pairs of ring-ditch houses are located in the upper left and right centre of the picture. These are a form of late prehistoric house in which scoops have been made in the interiors around the base of the walls, possibly to help in the over-wintering of cattle. Three linear stony banks, defining rough fields, and scattered small cairns indicate that this area was once cultivated. Although it is now under deep heather, the features are revealed by the snow-cover and strong sunlight. In the right centre is a curious key-hole shape which appears to be a rare form of animal enclosure. This site was discovered not long after the forestry ploughing, visible on the right.

78

79 New Kinord, Dinnet: a vertical view in winter of a quite different form of late prehistoric settlement represented by footings of stone. Of the features on the right, the two central circles, which have smaller circles within them, appear to represent house sites; a souterrain opens off the upper one and runs along the side of its neighbour. The three remaining circular enclosures have been interpreted as *kraals* or pens for cattle. The interiors of at least two of them have been significantly lowered (indicated by arcs of deep shadow). Traces of the curving stone wall of a drove-way can be seen above the houses. This settlement may date from roughly 2000 years ago.

80 Jericho, Colpy: the two small circular features, one snow-covered, the other standing clear, in the lower centre of the picture, are the stone footings of later prehistoric houses, often referred to as *hut circles*. The one on the right is located on the corner of a rectangular enclosure or field which runs downslope towards the modern stone dyke.

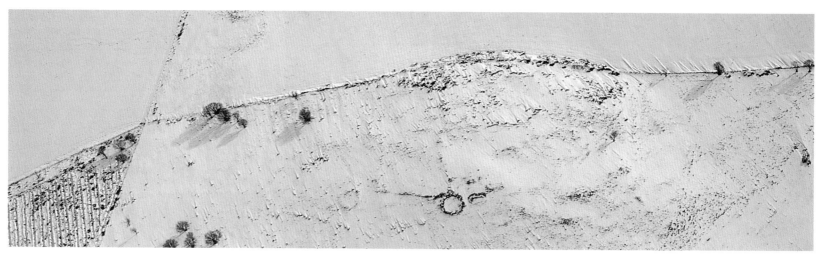

81 Windeye, Finzean. The modern forestry ploughing has been planned to avoid the low parallel stony banks in the centre of the picture, which show strip cultivation. A number of similar isolated examples of strip cultivation have been discovered on Deeside. At present they cannot be dated precisely. Modern attempts to cultivate this area can be seen near the top of the picture, at right angles to the banks.

82 Haughend, Finzean: a first-millennium BC, or earlier, farm revealed by a perfect combination of snow and angled sunlight. There is a hut circle in the bottom left and another in the upper centre, forward of the end of the ridge. A group of small cairns, or stone clearance heaps, gathered during cultivation, are clearly visible between the upper hut circle and the burn, as well as on the right of the picture.

83 The Ord, Balrownie, Strachan: another upland field system made comprehensible through a winter photograph. The two contrasting current land uses are clear, with the grouse moor's burnt strips above the boundary and rough grazing in the lower half. (The smoothed strip on the left is the track of a gas pipeline.) The centre of the picture bears an intensive pattern of small cairns and field banks created by the early farmers. In the upper right, clearance has been more complete and a single rectangular field containing a hut circle can be seen.

84 Kinord, Dinnet: an example of the very fine detail that can be recorded in winter flying. As well as the banks and small cairns of a later prehistoric field system, the very subdued ridges of "cord-rig" cultivation can be discerned in the lower half of the picture. Very few such 2500-year-old fields survive so well in eastern Scotland.

85 Deskry Hill, Strathdon. A complex sequence of events, presumptively of the first millennium BC, can be reconstructed from this winter shot. The earliest feature appears to be the faint traces of a circular house, scooped into the hillside, centre right. This is overlaid by cord-rig cultivation which runs uphill and under the prominent stony banks. These banks, and the hut circle which can be clearly seen, centre left, appear to relate to a re-organisation of the hillside, involving gathering stones into parallel and diagonal banks. The final phase of (? prehistoric) use is represented by the more prominent, narrow cultivation rigs which occupy the left-hand enclosure and overlie the upper arc of the hut circle. (A modern track has been bulldozed along the bottom of the slope.)

85
•
84•

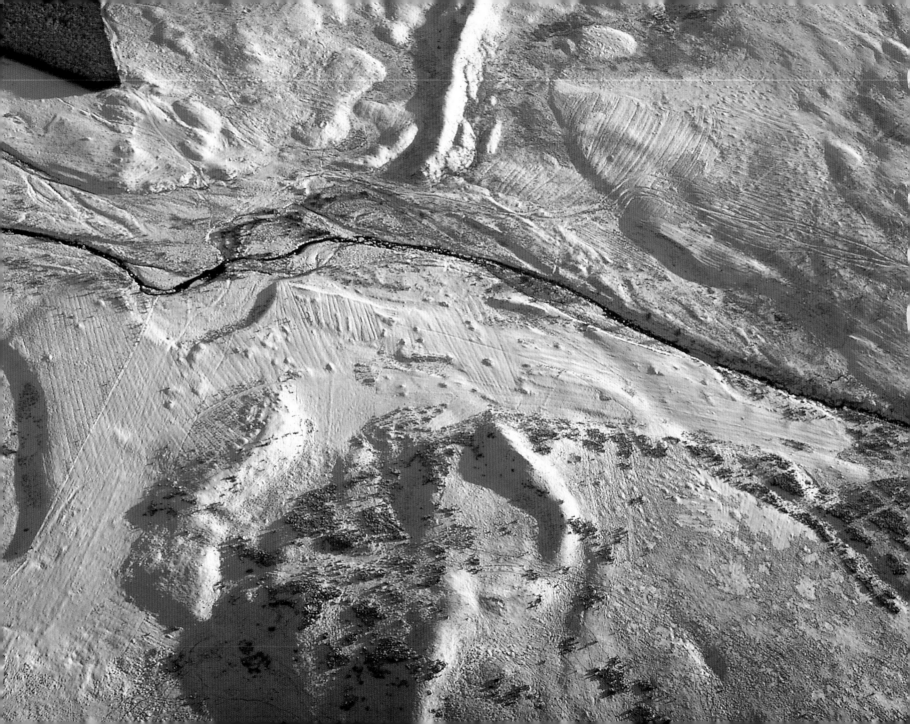

86 Water of Aven, Finzean: traces of rig cultivation of different types and date stand out owing to snow cover combined with strong sun. The dramatic humpback running down to the burn in the upper centre and continuing as a curved ridge, lower centre, is the remains of an esker, or glacial ridge. In the centre and left are traces of narrow or cord-rig cultivation and small clearance cairns. There is more rig, also of uncertain date, across the burn.

65

88 Hindstones, New Aberdour: the circular bank, which is all that survives of a Bronze-Age cairn, can be seen, surrounded by a later enclosure wall. As many as 15 other cairns have been recorded from the vicinity of this cairn, which is thus the sole survivor of an extensive Bronze-Age cemetery of c4000 years ago.

87 Bucharn, Finzean: a very substantial late Neolithic or early Bronze-Age burial cairn surrounded by a berm or platform which has been enhanced by the creation of the modern field. The low pile of stones to the immediate right of the cairn is modern clearance. The footings of a post-medieval longhouse are visible bottom right.

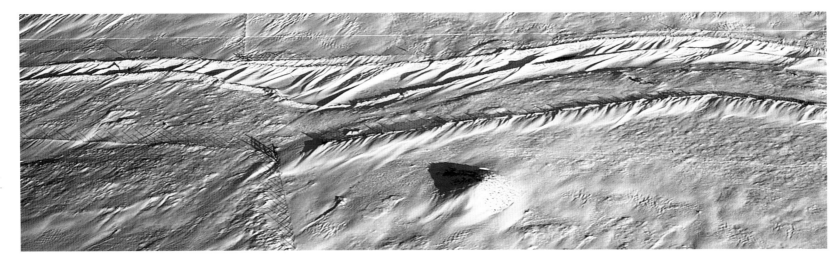

89 Cairn o'Mount in winter 1985. The B974 road, which takes its popular name from the Bronze-Age cairn at its summit (centre), is well and truly blocked.

90 Cairn Mude, Lumphanan. Forestry ploughing surrounds two early burial sites. The roughly oval mound at left centre may be an early form of burial cairn (perhaps as early as 5000 years ago). The irregular circular cairn, Cairn Mude, in centre right, was erected on this prominent hill shoulder some 4000 years ago.

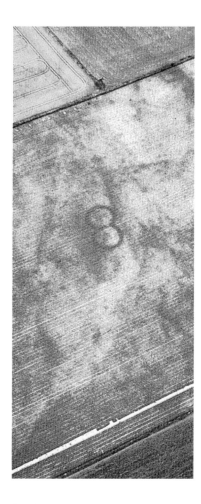

94 Kintocher, Craigievar: broad circular trace, with possible entrance gap on the left.

93 Kincraigie, Tarland: single trace of a broad circular ditch.

92 Mains of Melrose, Gardenstown: thin circular cropmark of a narrow ditch.

91 Shannocks, Turriff: early cropmark of two contiguous ring ditches.

When the prehistoric burial was made beneath an earth- or turf-mound or barrow its truncation or complete removal by subsequent ploughing was relatively easy. The ditches from which such barrows were quarried can, however, survive as cropmarks, called ring ditches.

92.
•91

94
93••90

89•

95 Boat of Hatton, Fintray; a truly massive ring ditch on a ridge immediately above the River Don. It forms part of a complex late-Neolithic ceremonial landscape as it lies beside the rare cursus monument shown on page 72.

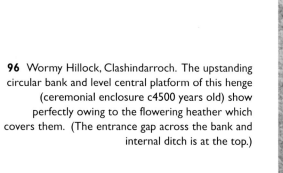

96 Wormy Hillock, Clashindarroch. The upstanding circular bank and level central platform of this henge (ceremonial enclosure c4500 years old) show perfectly owing to the flowering heather which covers them. (The entrance gap across the bank and internal ditch is at the top.)

97 Quarry Wood, Elgin. Clearance of the wood around this ditched enclosure or henge in 1991 reveals its plan. Bracken fills the central circular area and follows the circuit of the bank which lies outside the ditch. The existence of an inner bank (which might indicate that this was a defended site rather than a henge monument) has been disputed.

97•

96•

95•

98 Dilly Hill, Inverurie: a ploughed-out henge monument (c2500 BC), shown as an early cropmark of two concentric ditches. The outer trace is broader than the inner one. There may be two entrances: one is visible at top left, but the opposing one at the bottom right is less certain.

99 Broomend of Crichie, Port Elphinstone, Inverurie. This henge monument, with its outer bank and two opposed entrance causeways leading to a circular platform, is an upstanding version of the Dilly Hill cropmark. In the middle of the third millennium BC it was the centre of a ceremonial landscape. The small green patch, centre right, surrounds a standing stone, which is one of three survivors of a processional avenue consisting of 18 pairs of stones running towards (or from) the River Don. The stones of this avenue were blown up last century by *zealous agriculturalists*.

100 Standing Stones of Cullerlie, Garlogie.
A diminutive stone circle of the second millennium
BC, surrounding eight small burial cairns.

101 Loanhead of Daviot: a classic Aberdeenshire
recumbent stone circle (the recumbent is on the
right). When it was built in the third millennium BC
there was no cairn within the circle, the centre
being left clear for people to congregate in.
The prominent cairn within the central space was
added c4000 years ago when the site was
converted to use for burials. The two faint arcs
above the circle are the remains of an enclosed
cremation cemetery of the second millennium BC.

101.
98 . . 99
100 .

102 Fintray, Gordon. Dramatic late afternoon sun on summer cereal crops reveals the cropmark of a cursus, an extremely rare form of Neolithic monument, c3000 BC. It is formed from three contiguous rectilinear compartments defined by massive post-pits, seen most clearly at the eastern (left-hand) end. The cursus may have been built in two or more phases as the segments have differing alignments and varying tonal values in this photograph. (The central one is the most coherent.) The broad axis of the cursus is NW/SE. Such monuments are very rarely found, although features of this Fintray example are to be found at two sites in Angus. This monument is perched on a gravel ridge above several prominent bends in the River Don (which is out of shot at the top of the picture). Such cursuses can stretch for several miles; although their purpose is obscure, they may have been ceremonial- or processional- ways associated with funerals.

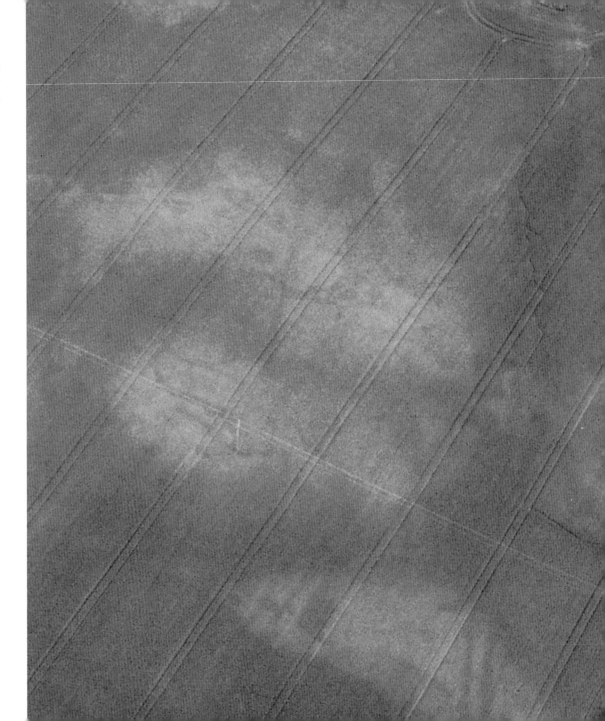

103 Purlieknowe, Kinneff. A cursus monument in the Mearns represented by two faint rectilinear cropmarks set end to end.

104 Standingstones, Roseisle, Moray. This sub-rectangular parchmark of an enclosure in the middle of the field was photographed in the very dry summer of 1989. It appears to represent a mortuary enclosure of the fourth millennium BC. Its discovery is consistent with 19th-century records of extensive discoveries of Neolithic pottery and burials in this area.

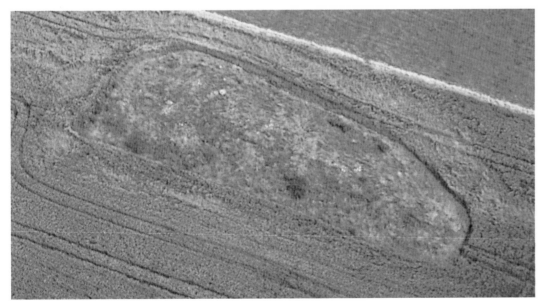

105 Gourdon long cairn: near-vertical view of a substantial elongated mound of earth and stones, erected c6000 years ago as a monument to the ancestors of the first farmers who occupied the surrounding hillslopes above the sea.

106 Den of Boddam, Peterhead. The heather-covered slopes above the mill dam were not taken into agriculture and therefore retain the pock-marking of 5000 year-old flint mines. More than 450 pits have been identified. Excavations by Alan Saville for the National Museums of Scotland (with assistance from Grampian Regional Council) have established that this was an extremely rare production-centre of flint for tool-making in the late third millennium BC.

107 Skelmuir Hill. Close aerial view of Alan Saville's re-excavation, 1994, for the National Museums of Scotland, of the 5000 year-old flint quarries dug to exploit the deposits of flint gravels in this area of Buchan.

110 Balbridie remains visible as a cropmark, although fully excavated, under appropriate conditions. Taken 1995.

108 The 6000 year-old timber hall at Balbridie, Deeside, under excavation in 1979. The site was revealed by aerial photography carried out by the Royal Commission on the Ancient and Historical Monuments of Scotland during the drought of 1976. This photograph shows the excavations conducted by Dr Ian Ralston, in which the bedding trench for the outer wall timbers and the lines of post-holes for internal timbers are visible.

109 Wester Fintray: on a gravel ridge in the square field in the centre of the picture, above the River Don, are traces of a circular enclosure which may contain signs of a timber hall, conceivably of Neolithic date. It forms part of the extensive, early prehistoric, cropmark landscape of the lower Don, also shown on pages 68 and 72.

111 Bellie, Fochabers. Running across one of the haughs of the River Spey, a line of dark dots, growing fainter in the distance, indicates the substantial post-pits of a massive land division of c5000 years ago. (The prominent frond-like, dark green marks are the remains of ancient flood channels.)